"What I like about being an editor is that it expands your knowledge and heightens your discrimination. Each book takes you down another path. Hopefully, some of them move people and some of them do some good."

"There are many ways to enlarge your child's world. Love of books is the best of all."

"To me a wonderful book is one that takes me on a journey into something I didn't know before."

"If you produce one book, you will have done something wonderful in your life."

Jackie

and the Books She Loved

Written by
Ronni Diamondstein

Illustrated by
Bats Langley

Sky Pony Press
New York

Sky Pony Press books may be purchased in bulk at special discounts for sales promotion, corporate gifts, fund-raising, or educational purposes. Special editions can also be created to specifications. For details, contact the Special Sales Department, Sky Pony Press, 307 West 36th Street, 11th Floor, New York, NY 10018 or info@skyhorsepublishing.com.

Sky Pony® is a registered trademark of Skyhorse Publishing, Inc.®, a Delaware corporation.

Visit our website at www.skyponypress.com.

10 9 8 7 6 5 4 3 2 1

Manufactured in China, May 2023
This product conforms to CPSIA 2008
Library of Congress Cataloging-in-Publication Data is available on file.

Jacket design by Bats Langley and Kai Texel
Jacket illustrations by Bats Langley
Edited by Nicole Frail
Typeset by Kate Hatcher

Print ISBN: 978-1-5107-7642-5
Ebook ISBN: 978-1-5107-7644-9

"If you produce one book, you will have done
something wonderful in your life."
—Jacqueline Kennedy Onassis

For Elizabeth Hall and everyone who loves books
and the joy of reading.

With much gratitude to Ambassador Caroline
Kennedy for her permission to reproduce the text
of the poem "Sea Joy."—RD

For the Clark-Spear family: Amy, Wally, my
husband Nicholas, Damaris, Benjamin, and Rachel.
You've shown me many wonderful things and have taken
me on many adventures, especially Martha's Vineyard,
one of Jackie's favorite places. —BL

Little Jackie Bouvier learned to read at an early age. She kept her books in a pair of bookcases that her mother had given her for Christmas. She started a library of her own—with many about ballet!—and filled the shelves in no time.

Sometimes, when Jackie was supposed to be napping, she would spend time in the guest room, where the grown-up books were kept, and sat on the windowsill reading.

Jackie had a vivid imagination and told people that a brown bear lived in her bedroom. She wrote and illustrated stories and poems, often about the family animals.

There was "The Adventures of George Woofty, Esq.," about a spirited terrier, and a funny biography of General de Gaulle, a bored and blasé black poodle.

Her mother collected Jackie's early writings, each piece in Jackie's firm, ornamental handwriting and bordered with a drawing. The stories, on thick, white notepaper, were tied together with bits of ribbon, or brightly colored string.

Every Wednesday after her dance class, Jackie visited her Grampy Jack Bouvier in his New York City apartment. The two would often memorize poems together, and he encouraged her to write her own. One of the poems she wrote was titled "Sea Joy."

When I go down by the sandy shore
I can think of nothing I want more
Than to live by the booming blue sea
As the seagulls flutter round about me
I can run about—when the tide is out
With the wind and the sand and the sea all about
And the seagulls are swirling and diving for fish
Oh-to live by the sea is my only wish.

Jacqueline Bouvier—1939

Jackie wrote birthday poems to her mother and father, and for family anniversaries, but Jackie always loved reading the best.

When she was fifteen, Jackie went off to Miss Porter's, an all-girls boarding school.

"Shh! I'm reading!" she would tell her roommate, Nancy, while the other girls were talking.

Jackie often could be found in her room reading and writing poetry, just as she had as a child. She even wrote stories and poems for the school newspaper.

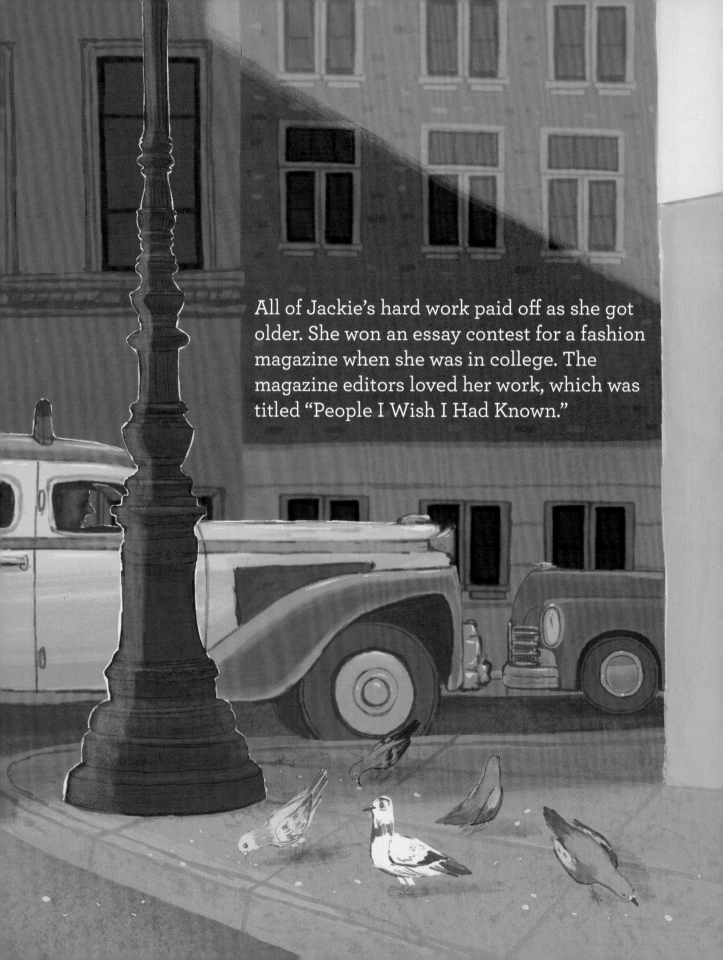

All of Jackie's hard work paid off as she got older. She won an essay contest for a fashion magazine when she was in college. The magazine editors loved her work, which was titled "People I Wish I Had Known."

Jackie had always been interested in history and decided she wanted to know people better. She thought that journalism would be a good way to do that. So, as an adult, she took a job in Washington, D.C. with a popular newspaper and went around town asking questions and taking pictures of people.

She interviewed everyone from bus drivers and children to ballet dancers and VIPs, including her future husband, Senator John F. Kennedy.

A love of reading was something Jackie had in common with John Kennedy. They both loved books so much, that when she went to London for work, she came back with a super heavy suitcase jam-packed with books as a gift for him.

Jackie married John F. Kennedy. They enjoyed reading and even writing together.

Jackie encouraged him to write an award-winning book. Jackie helped do the research for this book and even wrote down parts of it on lined yellow paper.

Jackie's writing skills helped Senator Kennedy become president of the United States! The voters got to know him and his family through her weekly newspaper column, which helped him get the votes he needed.

When President Kennedy took office, Jackie became the nation's First Lady. She thought there should be something young people could take with them as a souvenir after visiting the White House, so she designed a White House Guidebook, which she also edited.

As a mother, she hoped that her love of books would inspire her children, Caroline and John, making them readers, too.

Sadly, President Kennedy died in 1963. After that, Jackie and her children eventually moved to New York City.

Jackie encouraged Caroline and John to read great writers and poets.

And as she had done as a child with her Grampy Jack, for each birthday or holiday, Caroline and John would write or choose a poem for their mother, illustrate it, and paste it in a special scrapbook.

In 1975, Jackie got her first job in publishing—a perfect fit for a fan of reading and writing. She became a consulting editor for a publisher but refused any special treatment. In her small, windowless office, she answered the phone and sat on the floor, laying out photos.

In the summertime, she would work from her home on the island of Martha's Vineyard.

Even though she was very famous, for Jackie, the author was the true star of every book. She made sure to stay in the background and let her authors shine.

Jackie especially enjoyed editing books by young women writers. Many of her books addressed women's contributions to history. Jackie was ahead of her time.

During her career in publishing, Jackie edited books for children of all ages, including whimsical tales, books about ballet, modern dance, Hollywood, French writers, pop stars, different cultures, and art. All were the things Jackie loved.

She edited nearly one hundred books, many of which were bestsellers. She loved having a career and showing her children how important it is to have work you are passionate about.

Jacqueline Bouvier Kennedy Onassis had done many wonderful things in her life. She was most famous for being the First Lady of the United States, the wife and widow of President John F. Kennedy. But she made her mark as an editor.

A love of literature guided her life. The books that she read and that she edited were her story. She never wanted to write a memoir; however, now her books are her legacy and have painted her self-portrait.

Timeline

1929—Jacqueline Lee Bouvier is born in Southampton, New York, to Janet and Jack Bouvier on July 28

1933—Five-year-old Jackie and her mother, Janet, win Third Prize in the Family Class at the East Hampton Horse Show

1935—Jackie begins her education at Miss Chapin's School in New York City

1949—Jackie begins a year of study in France at the Sorbonne in Paris and University of Grenoble

1951— Jackie and her sister Lee spend the summer in Europe and they create a scrapbook about their adventures for their mother titled, "One Special Summer"

1952—Jackie meets Senator John F. Kennedy

1953—Jackie covers the coronation of Queen Elizabeth II in the United Kingdom

Jackie marries John F. Kennedy on September 12

1957—Jackie gives birth to a daughter, Caroline, on November 27

1960—Jackie gives birth to a son, John Fitzgerald Kennedy Jr., on November 25

1961—John F. Kennedy is inaugurated on January 20 in Washington, D.C.

Jackie begins the White House restoration

1963—Jackie accompanies President Kennedy to Dallas, Texas where he is assassinated on November 22

Jackie leads the nation in mourning at President Kennedy's funeral on November 25

1964—Jackie and her children move to New York City

1968—Jackie marries Aristotle Onassis

1975—Aristotle Onassis dies

Jackie takes a job as consulting editor at Viking Press

1978—Jackie begins work as Associate Editor at Doubleday Publishing

1979—The John F. Kennedy Library and Museum officially opens

1994—Jackie dies in her home in Manhattan on May 19

A Note from the Author

I was eight years old when Jacqueline Kennedy became the First Lady of the United States. As her husband President John F. Kennedy did so much to change the spirit in America, she did so much to change the White House and the role of the First Lady. I was fascinated by her style and grace, and I admired how she carried herself upon the assassination of her husband in 1963. Jackie led the nation with such dignity. She cared about history, and in her grief, reached out to the Library of Congress for the archives of the funeral of Abraham Lincoln, another beloved slain President. Like President Lincoln's funeral procession, a riderless horse symbolizing a leader who will lead no more followed Kennedy's casket.

Jackie was so precocious that she was reading the Russian author Chekov at age six, and the Civil War classic *Gone with the Wind* at age eleven. The book she loved most as a child was *The Mowgli Stories* by Rudyard Kipling. As a teen, she loved the poetry of Lord Byron; she read his poems and got to know him better by reading a biography about him.

Her grandfather Bouvier encouraged her writing, and when Jackie visited him in his country home on Long Island, the two would critique the editorials he published in the *East Hampton Star*. She was such a talented writer that one of her professors expected Jackie to write a book one day.

When Jackie won the *Vogue* magazine Prix de Paris her senior year of college, the editors were intrigued by her choice of people for the essay, *People I Wish I Had Known*. They were Diaghilev, a Russian ballet dancer; Oscar Wilde, a British author; and Charles Baudelaire, a French poet. Although Jackie won the contest, she chose not to accept the prize, which would've meant living in Paris for six months.

After college, she took a job in Washington, D.C. at the *Washington Times-Herald* as the "Inquiring Camera Girl" and interviewed her future husband, Senator John Kennedy, among others. In 1953, she went to London to cover Queen Elizabeth's coronation, and when she returned home, Senator Kennedy proposed. They married in September.

Jackie loved books and writing so much that when her husband was recuperating from back surgery, she encouraged him to write his Pulitzer Prize–winning book, *Profiles in Courage*. And she used her writing skills to help his presidential political campaign by writing a weekly newspaper column, *Campaign Wife*.

A handmaiden of beauty, Jackie became a fashion icon when she stepped onto the world stage as the First Lady of the United States on January 20, 1961. Her first project as First Lady was to refurbish the White House. In 1962, she was the first First Lady to win an Emmy Award for "The Tour of the White House." She hosted many cultural events at the White House, among them a romantic evening of Elizabethan poetry and music to which she invited one of her high school English teachers who had inspired her. And Jackie even brought the *Mona Lisa* to the United States and had a behind-the-scenes responsibility for bringing Egypt's *Temple of Dendur* to the Metropolitan Museum of Art.

After the devastating assassination of President Kennedy, Jackie was on her own and eventually moved to New York with her children, Caroline and John. She began to plan the John F. Kennedy Presidential Library and Museum in Boston.

Jackie loved literature and language and had a passion for poetry. She taught Caroline and John her favorite poems and encouraged them to discover poems on their own.

When her children were teenagers, Jackie decided it was time to go back to work. Books were so much a part of her life that it is no surprise she pursued publishing. She got her first job as a consulting editor at Viking Press in 1975 and then moved on to Doubleday in 1978 as an associate and then senior editor.

In 1979, when interviewed by Gloria Steinem for *Ms.* magazine about why women work, Jackie told Steinem, "I think that people who work themselves have respect for the work of others. I remember a taxi driver who took me to the office. He said, 'Lady, you work, and you don't *have* to?' I said yes. He turned around and said, 'I think that's great!'"

The first book she edited was *Remember the Ladies: Women in America*, a companion book to an American Bicentennial traveling exhibition of the role of women in the eighteenth century. She also edited a novel about Sally Hemings that gave voice to one of Thomas Jefferson's slaves.

She edited books for children of all ages, including whimsical tales by singer and songwriter Carly Simon and Peter Sís's book about his childhood in Prague, Czechoslovakia. There were books about classic ballet, modern dance, Hollywood, and pop star Michael Jackson's *Moonwalk*, as well as art books like *In the Russian Style*, an illustrated book on the clothing and artifacts from Czarist Russia.

In another of her very rare interviews she said, "I'm drawn to books that are out of our regular experience. Books of other cultures, ancient histories. I'm fascinated by hearing artists talk about their craft."

She encouraged writers and made all her authors feel special.

In 1980, she contributed to an anthology called *Books I Read when I was Young; The Favorite Books of Famous People* published by the National Council of Teachers of English.

"Read for escape, read for adventure, read for romance, but read the great writers . . .

Read Edgar Allan Poe, Jack London, Jules Verne, Ernest Hemingway. And read poetry—in whatever anthology your school gives you . . . If you read, you may want to write . . .

Writing helps you to express your deepest feelings. Once you can express yourself you can tell the world what you want from it or how you would like to change it. All the changes in the world, for good or evil, were first brought about by words."

In 1994, Jackie was diagnosed with non-Hodgkin's lymphoma. She passed away on May 19, 1994. Her son, John F. Kennedy Jr., spoke to the crowd of press and fans outside her Fifth Avenue apartment in New York City.

"Last night, at around ten-fifteen, my mother passed on. She was surrounded by her friends and her family and her books and the people and the things that she loved. And she did it in her own way and in her own terms, and we all feel lucky for that and now she is in God's hands."

The books Jackie edited reflect her taste, her passions, and her recollections. She was more than one of the most famous women in the world and a First Lady. Her achievements as an editor were a testament to who she was as a person. As a writer and librarian, I have always been fascinated by her love of books and her career as an editor. I am honored to share this story with young people. This book is a tribute to Jackie.

A Representative Selection of the Books
Edited by Jacqueline Kennedy Onassis

Bernier, Olivier. *Secrets of Marie Antoinette: By Marie Antoinette, Queen Consort of Louis, XVI, King of France*. Garden City, N.Y.: Doubleday, 1985.

Campbell, Joseph. *The Power of Myth*. With Bill Moyers. Edited by Betty Sue Flowers. New York: Doubleday, 1988.

Chase-Riboud, Barbara. *Sally Hemings: A Novel*. New York: Viking, 1979.

De Pauw, Linda and Conover Hunt. *Remember the Ladies: Women in America 1750-1815*. With the assistance of Miriam Schneir. New York: Viking/Pilgrim, 1976.

Dickinson, Emily. *Skies in Blossom: The Nature Poetry of Emily Dickinson*. Edited by Jonathan Cott, illustrations by Mary Frank. New York: Doubleday, 1995.

Jackson, Michael. *Moonwalk*. New York: Doubleday, 1988.

Jhabvala, Ruth Prawer. *Shards of Memory*. New York: Doubleday, 1995.

Kirkland, Gelsey. *The Little Ballerina and Her Dancing Horse*. With Greg Lawrence. Illustrated by Jacqueline Rogers. New York: Doubleday, 1993.

Moyers, Bill D. *A World of Ideas Conversations with Thoughtful Men and Women About American Life Today and the Ideas Shaping Our Future*. With by Betty Sue Flowers. New York: Doubleday, 1989.

Onassis, Jacqueline, ed. *In the Russian Style*. With the cooperation of the Metropolitan Museum of Art. Introduction by Audrey Kennett, designed by Bryan Holme. New York: Viking, 1976.

Previn, André. *No Minor Chords: My Days in Hollywood*. New York: Doubleday, 1991.

Simon, Carly. *Amy the Dancing Bear*. Illustrated by Margot Datz. New York: Doubleday, 1989.

Simon, Paul. *At the Zoo*. Illustrated by Valérie Michaut. New York: Doubleday,1991.

Sís, Peter. *The Three Golden Keys*. New York: Doubleday, 1994.

Turbeville, Deborah. *Unseen Versailles*. Introduction by Louis Auchincloss. Garden City, N.Y.: Doubleday, 1981.

Vreeland, Diana. *Allure*. With Christopher Hemphill. Garden City, N.Y.: Doubleday, 1980.

West, Dorothy. *The Wedding*. New York: Doubleday, 1995.

Zvorykin, Boris. *The Firebird and Other Russian Fairy Tales*. Edited with an introduction by Jacqueline Onassis. New York: Viking, 1978.

Selected Sources

Adler, Bill (Ed.) *The Eloquent Jacqueline Kennedy Onassis: A Portrait in Her Own Words.* New York: William Morrow, 2004.

Adler, Bill (Ed.) *The Uncommon Wisdom of Jacqueline Kennedy Onassis: A Portrait in Her Own Words.* New York: Carol Publishing Group, 1994.

Anthony, Carl Sferrazza. *As We Remember Her: Jacqueline Kennedy Onassis in the Words of Her Family and Friends.* New York: Harper Collins, 1977.

Baker, John F. "Editors at Work: Star Behind the Scenes (interview with Jacqueline Kennedy Onassis.)" *Publishers Weekly*, April 19, 1993.

Davis, John H. *Jacqueline Bouvier: An Intimate Memoir.* New York: John Wiley & Sons, Inc., 1996.

Kennedy, Caroline. *The Best-Loved Poems of Jacqueline Kenney Onassis.* New York: Hyperion, 2001.

Kuhn, William. *Reading Jackie: Her Autobiography in Books.* New York: Doubleday, 2010.

"Life of Jacqueline B. Kennedy." John F. Kennedy Presidential Library and Museum website. https://www.jfklibrary.org/learn/about-jfk/life-of-jacqueline-b-kennedy

National Council of Teachers of English. *Books I Read When I Was Young: The Favorite Books of Famous People.* Edited by Bernice Cullinan. Avon Books, January 1, 1980.

Steinem, Gloria. "On Jacqueline Kennedy Onassis." *Ms.* March 1979.

Thayer, Mary Van Rensselaer. *Jacqueline Bouvier Kennedy.* Garden City, NY: Doubleday & Company, Inc., 1961.

Source Credits

All quotations are from Adler, Bill (Ed.) *The Eloquent Jacqueline Kennedy Onassis: A Portrait in Her Own Words*. New York: William Morrow, 2004, and Adler, Bill (Ed.) *The Uncommon Wisdom of Jacqueline Kennedy Onassis: A Portrait in Her Own Words*. New York: Carol Publishing Group, 1994, with the exception of "A taxi driver... 'I think that's great!'" and "What I like best about being an editor..." which are from Steinem, Gloria. "On Jacqueline Kennedy Onassis." *Ms.* March 1979, "I'm drawn to books . . . artists talk about their craft," and "To me a wonderful book is . . . know before," which are from Baker, John F. "Editors at Work: Star Behind the Scenes (interview with Jacqueline Kennedy Onassis)" *Publishers Weekly*, April 19, 1993.

About the Author

© Randi Childs

Ronni Diamondstein spent her life surrounded by books and immersed in the world of children's literature. As a school library media specialist and teacher of gifted and talented students in the United States and abroad, Ronni nurtured her students' creativity by sharing her love of reading with them. Ronni is a graduate of Syracuse University. She attended Bread Loaf Writers' Conference and led writing workshops and open mics to encourage people of all ages to tell their stories. Ronni served on the Board of the Chappaqua Children's Book Festival and is a Past President of the Chappaqua Library Board of Trustees. *Jackie and the Books She Loved* is her debut picture book. Ronni lives in Chappaqua, New York with her toy poodle, Maggie Mae.

About the Illustrator

© Nicholas Clark-Spear

Bats Langley is a painter, sculptor, writer, illustrator, toy designer, and creator of many things. Bats, a Rhode Island School of Design (RISD) grad, frequently contributes illustrations for the covers and interiors of *Scholastic*, *Spider*, *Ladybug*, and *Cricket* magazines. His art has been shown in galleries across the United States and the world. He illustrated *Groggle's Monster Valentine* and *Groggle's Monster Halloween* and was the author/illustrator of *Alice's Adventures in #Wonderland*. Bats created the cover art for *Scary Stories to Tell on The Pod*, a podcast hosted by *SNL* head writer Anna Drezen and TV writer Andrew Farmer. He lives with his husband, Nicholas, on the island of Manhattan.

"I'm drawn to books that are out of our regular experience. Books of other cultures, ancient histories. I'm fascinated by hearing artists talk about their craft."

"I always wanted to be a writer. . . . Like a lot of people, I dreamed of writing the Great American Novel."

"I'd majored in literature, I had many friends in publishing, I love books, I've known writers all my life."

"Like everybody else, I have to work my way up to an office with a window."